Published by Creative Education
123 South Broad Street, Mankato, Minnesota 56001
Creative Education is an imprint of The Creative Company

Designed by Stephanie Blumenthal
Production Design by Melinda Belter

Photographs by John Elk III, Robert Fried, Bob McKeever, Brian Parker,
Anthony Russo, Eugene G. Schulz

Library of Congress Cataloging-in-Publication Data

Halfmann, Janet.
Greek temples / by Janet Halfmann
p. cm. — (Designing the future)
Includes index
Summary: Examines the history, design, construction, and uses of Greek temples
and describes some notable examples.
ISBN 0-88682-654-3
1. Temples—Greece—Juvenile literature. [1. Temples—Greece.] I. Title. II. Series.
NA275.H28   1999
726'.1208—dc21   98-18206

First Edition

2 4 6 8 9 7 5 3 1

GREEK TEMPLES

JANET HALFMANN

CREATIVE EDUCATION

Every morning, the donkey ran back to the building site in ancient Greece even though it didn't have to be there. It had worked hard for years carting heavy marble blocks up the steep hill of the Acropolis. The animal's service complete, it was old and was free to spend its days resting and eating grass. But each day, it returned to trot alongside its former teammates, as if to encourage and cheer them on. The ancient writer Plutarch tells the story of this spirited donkey. It was one of thousands of animals and people working

Remains of the Zeus altar

together about 2,500 years ago to build a temple for a magnificent statue in celebration of a goddess.

The great Greek sculptor Phidias was creating an ivory and gold statue of Athena Parthenos (Athena the Warrior Maiden), the goddess of wisdom. Athena was also the war goddess, but she was not so much a

According to legend, a fight between two rams led to the discovery of marble. One of the ram's horns hit the mountainside, chipping off a piece of stone with a loud ring. The shepherd rushed to show others the valuable discovery he had made.

fighter as a wise adviser. Her temple would come to be known as the Parthenon, which to this day dominates the Acropolis in Athens, the capital of modern-day Greece.

The ancient Greeks believed in many gods and goddesses. The gods behaved much like ordinary people, but they had great wisdom.

Below, Pronaos frieze; opposite, the Medusa frieze at Hadrian's Temple at Ephesus

They were wiser, more cunning, and more powerful.

They also lived forever. The gods controlled nature and

people's fate. There were 12 main gods, known as the

Olympians. Some of the most famous included Zeus,

Athena, Poseidon, and Apollo.

Greek temples were houses for these gods,

often built in places that people believed were special

to their gods. The Acropolis, or "high city," in Athens

is one such place.

Entering a temple, a visitor would find a statue

Temple of Zeus

of a god or goddess at the end of a long, dark room. A row of columns ran down the center of the room or along both sides. A Greek of the time might have visited the temple to thank the god for a favor and leave a gift.

The inside of a temple wasn't a gathering place for worship, like churches and sacred buildings of today. Worship services were held outside on an altar. The temple instead protected the statue of the god from the weather.

Sometimes a temple was a gift to a god or goddess for a favor, such as winning a war. The Parthenon was a gift to Athena for the Greeks' victory in the Persian Wars.

The Greeks believed that sports contests pleased their gods. Athletes from all over Greece came to compete at Olympia, near the large Temple of Zeus. Training tracks, baths, and a stadium surrounded the temple. The first Olympic Games were held in 776 B.C.

The construction of Greek temples followed four basic plans. The earliest temples date from the eighth century B.C. Their plan was simple, calling for one long room, known as the naos, and a porch in front supported by wooden columns.

The second plan called for porches at both ends because the Greeks liked things to look balanced,

Figures from the frieze of the Parthenon

The Hepaisteion overlooking the Athens agora

or symmetrical. The Temple of Athena Nike (Athena of Victory) on the Acropolis in Athens was built like this. It has a simple, delicate style, with four columns on the front and rear porches. To make the third temple style, the Greeks put a ring of columns, or peristyle, all around it. Called peripteral, this symmetrical plan for temples became the most popular. It had 11 to 18 columns on the sides, and usually six columns on the ends. The roof

W   I   N   G   S

The goddess Nike had wings so she could fly down to Earth to bring victory in battle. Today, the goddess's wing is represented by the Nike Swoosh, the logo of a well-known sportswear company.

Ionic columns of the temple of Athena Nike

A wall of the Acropolis

The design of temples was a reflection of a city-state's pride, wealth, and power. As city-states grew in size and the people amassed more money and property, the choice of building materials changed from wood and sun-dried mud bricks to more prestigious—and more expensive—limestone and marble.

A second room often was added to later temples. This area could be used to store gifts given to the gods. Generally, the buildings faced east so that

extended to the peristyle columns and created a covered walkway all around the temple. The Temple of Hephaestus in Athens is an example of this style.

A fourth plan, used by wealthy cities, had double peristyles. This type, called dipteral, usually had eight columns along the front. The splendid dipteral Temple of Artemis at Ephesus had an incredible 127 exterior columns.

C A R Y A T I D S

The Erechtheum is famous for its south porch, where six statues of maidens called caryatids serve as the porch's columns. The present statues are copies. The originals are in the British Museum and the Acropolis Museum.

A row of Doric columns

sunlight shining into the open doorway could fall on the statue. Windows in temples were rare.

Greek temples were built in two main orders, or styles: Doric and

Corinthian style column top

Ionic. A Doric temple has thick columns, with plain tops, called capitals. The decorated band, or frieze, above the columns has ridged stone panels that alter-

nate with plain or carved panels. The Parthenon and the Temple of Apollo at Corinth, built around 540 B.C., are examples of Doric temples.

An Ionic temple has slimmer columns, and its capitals are decorated with spiral shapes called volutes. Its frieze is not divided and is usually decorated. Though only part of a column and

Temple of Poseidon

Column sections at the Temple of Olympian

some of the foundation of the Temple of Hera at Samos still exist today, the second temple on the site was believed to be modeled after the magnificent Temple of Artemis, which was one of the Seven Wonders of the Ancient World.

A variation of the Ionic is the ornate Corinthian, which has capitals decorated with volutes and acanthus leaves. The Corinthian columns of the Temple of Olympian Zeus, built around 170 B.C., can still be seen in Athens today.

Most temples of the time were built of limestone, but building designers, or architects, were always looking for finer stone. They often used bright white marble dug from the mountains. Skilled craftsmen came from all over Greece to carry out the architects' plans. Quarry workers, stonemasons,

carpenters, metalworkers, model builders, painters, engravers, and road builders, as well as many unskilled laborers found work constructing temples. The workers used simple tools typically made of iron—picks, chisels, punches, and drills—and struck them with wooden hammers or mallets.

Cutting the marble blocks from the mountain took skill and hard work. First, the workers used mallets and chisels to outline the block to be cut. Then they hammered wooden wedges into the grooves. They

The Acropolis in Athens, Greece

Ionic columns along the Holy Road-via Tecta

poured water on the wedges to make the wood swell, cracking the marble. The blocks were then trimmed, leaving four knobs sticking out so the stones could be lifted into place at the building site. Even more difficult, the workers had to guide the stones down the steep, rocky mountain on sleds from heights of up to 3,000 feet (914 m).

Oxen then pulled the blocks on wagons, the largest stones requiring wagons with wheels 12 feet

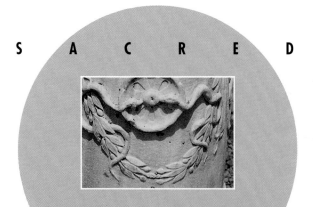

S A C R E D

In Greek mythology, Athena caused an olive tree to spring up. The people liked the olive tree so much that Zeus gave the city's protection to Athena.

Corinthian columns at the ruins of Corinth, Greece

19

Remains of the temple of Dionysus

(4 m) in diameter. It took 30 or 40 teams of oxen to pull them, and two days to make the trip. To build just one temple—the Parthenon in Athens —people and animals carted 22,000 tons (19,954 metric tons) of marble.

The Temple of Apollo at Bassae in southern Greece uses all three kinds of columns—Doric, Ionic, and Corinthian. This temple, built to thank Apollo for sparing the people from the plague, still stands. It can be found all alone on a small hill.

At the building site, skilled stonemasons smoothed the blocks to fit together perfectly, since no mortar was used. The peristyle columns were put up first. Each column was made up of many sections, each weighing up to 10 tons (9 metric tons). The workers heaved them into position using ropes, pulleys, and cranes, centering the sections above each other by wooden pegs. The fit was so perfect on both columns and walls that the seams could hardly be seen. Workers used iron clamps for fastening the blocks of the walls together.

Imported marble, used for statues, was also used for roof tiles. Because of its fine grain, the marble could be sliced into tiles only one inch (2.5 cm) thick. When the roof and blocks were in place, workers chiseled off the knobs and smoothed all of the surfaces. But the temple wasn't yet finished.

As the temples were going up, artists were busy carving the statue decorations. Sculptures of gods,

An armored torso from the Traian temple

Vaulting bottom galleries of the Traian temple

monsters, and Greek heroes adorned each side of the temple. The artists carved the frieze that ran around all four sides of the nao and statues for the triangle-shaped areas just under the roof, called pediments. The artists paid close attention to every detail, carefully finishing the back of each statue even though it wouldn't be seen once the figure was in place.

Then the artists painted the sculptures in bright colors. They painted the backgrounds in blue and the figures in black, red, and yellow. They added colored glass to highlight eyes. Some statues were even adorned in gold. The figure of Athena at the Parthenon included a robe covered in 2,500 pounds (1,135 kg) of gold worth 15 million dollars by current standards.

Today, the Parthenon is a ruin and the statue of Athena no longer exists, but it is still one of the world's most beautiful buildings. Though tourists are no longer allowed to enter the Parthenon, millions visit the area every year. Temples can be found throughout Greece and its islands and also in many places where the ancient Greeks settled, such as in southern Italy and Sicily. The Greek government continues to restore ancient buildings, and efforts are underway to decrease smog, a major threat to the temples. Sculptures seen at most temples today are only copies.

D E C O R A T I O N

Mosaics such as this one along the Currettes Road at Ephesus were commonly made to decorate walkways and walls of both temples and homes.

Little is left of ancient Greek structures

The originals were moved to museums long ago to keep pollution from turning them to dust.

Many temples could not be saved. The Temple of Zeus at Olympia was the largest Doric temple in Greece when completed in 456 B.C. It measured 210 feet (64 m) long, 91 feet (28 m) wide, and 65 feet (20 m) high.

A round Greek temple is called a tholos. The Tholos at Delphi, built around 390 B.C., had an outer ring of 20 Doric columns and an inner ring of 10 Corinthian columns. It was dedicated to Athena. Three of its outer columns have been restored, but the rest lies in ruin.

The temple was built of local shell limestone and had 102 lion-head waterspouts jutting from its marble roof. It housed a huge ivory and gold statue of Zeus—one of the Seven Wonders of the Ancient World—and the first Olympic Games took place there to honor Zeus. Today, only the foundation and scattered column

Detail of the roof of the Parthenon in Athens

The Tholos at Delphi

drums remain of this once-fantastic structure.

Pollution isn't the only danger to temples. Ancient landmarks are often intentionally damaged by people, or vandalized. The white marble columns of the Doric Temple of Poseidon at Sounion above the cliffs of the Aegean Sea have been a landmark for sailors since ancient times, but when the famous poet Byron carved his name on one of the columns in 1810, many other visitors did the same. The temple is now covered with signatures.

Most visitors to Greece, however, respect the ancient ruins. Perhaps nowhere else in the world can

Steps at the Asklepion Theater at Pergamon

people see as many temples in one place as in the former Greek colony of Agrigento, Sicily. The ruins include the temples of Hera, Concord, Hercules, Olympian Zeus, and Hephaestus. The temple of Concord (a modern name) is one of the best-preserved of all Greek temples.

Southern Italy's ancient city of Paestum is most famous for Doric temples that have survived from the city's period as a Greek colony. The well-preserved Temple of Poseidon was built in the fifth century B.C., and two other temples still in fair condition date back to the sixth century B.C.

The construction of these and other temples led

Remains of the Basilica at Ephesus

architects in other countries to imitate Greek design and style over the years. Many modern buildings around the world exhibit Greek temple design because architects admire the balance, harmony, order, and simple elegance of the Greek style.

The British Museum, which houses many of the sculptures from the Parthenon, was modeled after the Temple of Athena Polias at Priene in Asia Minor. The Lincoln Memorial in Washington, D. C., finished

Above and opposite, the Lincoln Memorial in Washington, D.C.

in 1922, is modeled after the Parthenon. Its architect, Henry Bacon, turned the classic Greek building design to its side, however, making the long side the front of the memorial. Its 36 exterior Doric columns represent the states in the Union at the time of Abraham Lincoln's death, and the frieze above the columns lists the names of 48 states. Alaska and Hawaii are represented with a plaque on the front steps.

N A S H V I L L E

The frieze of the Parthenon in Nashville, Tennessee, is painted in a style that closely resembles descriptions of the original at the Acropolis.

29

Sanctuary of Apollo at Delphi

In Nashville, Tennessee, stands a full-scale copy of the Parthenon. When it was built in 1897 for the state's Centennial Exposition, Nashville had the nickname "Athens of the South." The building was supposed to be temporary, but it proved so popular that it was left standing and rebuilt in concrete in 1920. It even has a 42-foot (13 m) statue of Athena created by a Nashville sculptor.

Greek temple design can be seen in state-houses, banks, libraries, schools, churches, and also in houses, large and small. Houses range from mansions with large columned porches to ordinary houses with single columns on each side of the front door. While the Greek civilization may have died out long ago, the spirit of the Greek temple lives on in architectural designs all around the world.

Doric columns at the temple of Apollo, Corinth

I N D E X

The Celsus Library at Ephesus